Budgeting on a Dime

10 Steps to Financial Independence

DIANE TEGARDEN

Library of Congress Cataloging-in-Publication Data

Tegarden, Diane 1957–

Budgeting on a Dime: 10 Steps to Financial Independence/ Diane Tegarden. ISBN
0-9745369-6-2

1. Budgeting   2. Self Help   3. Finances   4. Do-It-Yourself

FireWalker Publications, Inc
3579 E. Foothill Blvd. #322
Pasadena, CA 91107-3119

Editor: Camille DeSalme
Interior Design: Delaine Ulmer
Covert Art Design: Delaine Ulmer

Printed in the United States by Lightning Source Inc.

Acknowledgements

I'd like to thank all the students who have taken my class "Budgeting on a Dime" for their hard work, encouragement and great questions.

I want to send a shout-out to my Ryze.com buddies from my "Wordmeisters, Poets and Writers-Unite!" network. They are a great bunch of people who are supportive, caring and always there with a receptive ear.

Thank you to my manuscript readers: Diane Stephenson and Marsha Eastwood for their helpful comments, editing tips, reviews and insights.

I'm sending out lots of gratitude to my fantastic book designer, Delaine Ulmer, for her attention to detail, experience and knack for perfection in both interior and exterior book design.

Finally, I'd like to thank my clever and ever-patient editor, Camille DeSalme!

Contents

Introduction

While it's true that our country is suffering from a deep recession, that's not the reason why I wrote this self-help book. I'm writing this book because although we are required to attend high school to learn basic life skills, there aren't many high schools that offer classes on how to manage your money.

People need to know that they can live on what they earn, they need to save for emergencies and they need to plan for the future. Not to mention having some fun along the way!

Most colleges don't offer basic money management as a general education class, unless you're going into business or planning to become a CPA. But every person who makes money needs to know how much they are spending, where they are spending it (what types of expenses) and where they are overspending.

With this book, you will learn what assets are, what your monthly expenditures are, and how you can reduce many areas of spending so you are living within your means.

It offers ways to eliminate credit card debt, tells how to set up a savings account, and even has a brief outline of retirement planning (although it is by no means comprehensive).

There's another good reason to manage your money wisely. According to an article by Alex Veiga of the Associated Press, the number one reason couples divorce or separate is financial problems. So if you can learn how to manage your money together, instead of fighting about it, you have a better chance of having a healthy relationship.

May you never thirst...for knowledge...for water...for love,

~Diane Tegarden

Chapter 1
Decide You Want
to Change Your Life!

Decide You WILL Change Your Financial Situation

Decide that you WILL change your financial situation. Henry Ford, the brilliant industrialist who created Ford Motor Company, said, "If you think you can do a thing or think you can't do a thing, you're right." This means you have to start any project with the belief that you can accomplish it, or you are working against yourself.

Many creative and successful people use PMA—Positive Mental Attitude—as a key ingredient to their own success. You have to feed yourself positive thoughts, make a plan to solve your financial problems, and then have the courage to follow your convictions.

Step through each phase, and take the slow and steady course. No one ever accomplished their goals instantly, so you have to give yourself enough time to succeed.

Did you know it took Thomas Edison 1,000 tries to get the first light bulb to work? As an inventor, Edison made 1,000 unsuccessful attempts at inventing the light bulb.

When a reporter asked, "How did it feel to fail 1,000 times?" Edison replied, "I didn't fail 1,000 times. The light bulb was an invention with 1,000 steps."

You have to be willing to fail, try again, succeed a little, fail a little, and keep on taking one step at a time toward your goal.

My Formula for Success: Vision, Energy, Focus

Vision: See what you want for your financial future; paint a vivid mental picture of it. Then make a plan of action on the steps you'll need to take to get there.

Energy: Take the steps you have outlined in order to get to your goal.

Focus: Don't give up. Remember, Thomas Edison made 1000 attempts before his first test light bulb lit up!

Ten Tips on How to Avoid Arguing About Money

1. Get a joint checking account.

If you are both putting your money into a joint checking account you both have a vested interest in keeping track of it and both know you're contributing to the finances.

2. Learn how to do your bank reconciliation.

Once a month, at the end of the month, reconcile your bank statement, so you know which checks haven't yet cleared (see chapter 2). Look at total deposits and total withdrawals on the statement, so you both know exactly how much money is going into and out of the account. This empowers you both with the knowledge of where you are spending your money.

3. At the beginning of the year, make a budget.

A budget gives you both guidelines on how much you need for necessaries, like rent, car insurance, car payments, food and utilities. You can then both agree on how much money is available for luxury items and discuss what those items may be. This will help you avoid overspending, and agreeing on these items supports you both to keep your word on what you spend.

4. Once a quarter, compare your outgoing spending with the budget.

This will alert you when you may be veering off course and help you keep on track with luxury spending.

5. Start saving for retirement with your first paycheck.

Instead of being fearful of living in poverty, start saving for retirement/emergencies by having small automatic payments transferred from your joint checking into your savings account every month.

6. Pay off your credit cards every month.

This practice can save you hundreds of dollars a year because you won't be paying interest fees on your purchases. Set a realistic limit on your credit card spending and pay off the balance with each statement.

7. Join a credit union.

By joining a credit union you can earn more money than if you have your checking or savings at a regular bank. Also, once you establish a relationship with your credit union, it will be easier to qualify for a loan, if you need, for example, emergency funds.

8. Set a limit on your Christmas spending.

Every year people get themselves into deep credit card debt at Christmas and are still paying off those debts when next December rolls around. Sit down and talk about whom you want to buy gifts for, and set realistic limits on the amount you will spend. Stick to it and you'll be much happier on New Year's Day.

9. Celebrate your financial victories.

No one wants to do all this work without a reward. Choose inexpensive ways to celebrate your financial willpower by going to a movie or out to eat once a quarter. Or use your imagination to think up new, inexpensive ways to celebrate your financial victories and you'll be more likely to keep up the good work.

10. Learn more.

If budgeting doesn't come naturally to you, or working with your finances seems too confusing, take some free/low-cost financial courses online or at a community college. Get some help learning how to balance your bank statement (ask someone at your bank if they can explain it), or find out how to set up a budget.

Chapter 2
Evaluate Your Assets

Assets Evaluation. Monthly Expense Form, Bank Reconciliation

Regardless of your financial worth, being clear about your financial status will EMPOWER you, although you must put some work into it. You may choose to use your lack of understanding of financial matters to prevent you from taking the next step, but if you truly want to be financially independent, don't use this as an excuse not to go forward.

Assets Evaluation

Begin the process by taking stock of your assets. Assets are items of value. They include the value of your house, rental property, pension plans, bank accounts, stocks, bonds, cars, businesses, antiques, life insurance, household furnishings, etc. You may be surprised, while making this list, by the actual value of what you own. When preparing this checklist, you should add any additional items you consider of value.

Please take the time to fill out the Assets Form on the next page now.

ASSETS FORM

Assets:

Cash in Checking Account	+$_____
Cash in Savings	+$_____
Dividends and Securities	+$_____
Cash Surrender Value of Life Insurance	+$_____
Cash Distributions from Business	+$_____
Value of Residences	+$_____
Value of Vehicles	+$_____
Retirement Plan Value	+$_____
Other Assets	+$_____
Other Income: Spousal Support/Alimony or Child Support	+$_____
TOTAL OF ALL ASSETS	**+$_____**

Liabilities:

Mortgage and Notes Payable	−$_____
Income Taxes Past Due	−$_____
Other Liabilities	−$_____
TOTAL OF ALL LIABILITIES	**−$_____**

Take the Total of All Assets and Subtract the Total of All Liabilities	$_____
= YOUR NET WORTH (+/−)	**$_____**

Monthly Living Expenses

Next, fill out the Total Now Column of the Monthly Living Expenses Worksheet. Your debts are commonly referred to as liabilities. These include the mortgage on your house, monthly rent on your apartment, car loans, credit card debt, lines of credit, lease commitments and any other debts.

After you read the sections on how to reduce some of your expenses, come back and fill in the Plan for Expense Reduction column.

MONTHLY LIVING EXPENSES WORKSHEET

Monthly Expense	Total Now	Plan for Expense Reduction	New Amount

Home Expenses

House Payment			
House Insurance			
Property Tax			
Other Expense			
Other Expense			
Subtotal			

Entertainment

NetFlix			
Internet			
Other Expense			
Other Expense			
Subtotal			

Food

Groceries			
Food Out			
Subtotal			

MONTHLY LIVING EXPENSES WORKSHEET *(con't.)*

Monthly Expense	Total Now	Plan for Expense Reduction	New Amount

Cars

Monthly Expense	Total Now	Plan for Expense Reduction	New Amount
Vehicle #1 Insurance			
Vehicle #2 Insurance			
Gas for #1			
Gas for #2			
Other Expense			
Other Expense			
Subtotal			

Utilities

Monthly Expense	Total Now	Plan for Expense Reduction	New Amount
Gas Company			
Phone: Landline			
Phone: Cell phone			
Other Utility Bill			
Electric & Refuse			
Water & Sewer			
Subtotal			

MONTHLY LIVING EXPENSES WORKSHEET *(con't.)*

Monthly Expense	Total Now	Plan for Expense Reduction	New Amount
Medical			
Health Insurance			
Health: Out of Pocket			
Dental Insurance			
Dental: Out of Pocket			
Massage/Chiro.			
Accupucture			
Eye Care/Glasses			
Other Expense			
Other Expense			
Subtotal			

Personal Care

Beauty/Barber			
Other Expense			
Other Expense			
Other Expense			
Subtotal			

MONTHLY LIVING EXPENSES WORKSHEET *(con't.)*

Monthly Expense	Total Now	Plan for Expense Reduction	New Amount
Hobbies			
Other Expense			
Subtotal			

Savings & Credit Card Debts

Credit Card #1			
Credit Card #2			
Savings			
Other Expense			
Subtotal			

Life Insurance & IRAs

Life Insurance #1			
Life Insurance #2			
Life Insurance #3			
IRA #1			
IRA #2			
Other Expense			
Subtotal			

MONTHLY LIVING EXPENSES WORKSHEET *(con't.)*

Monthly Expense	Total Now	Plan for Expense Reduction	New Amount
Miscellaneous/Other			
Other Expense			
Other Expense			
Other Expense			
Subtotal			

GRAND TOTAL EXPENSES			

HOW MUCH DO YOU NEED TO REDUCE YOUR MONTHLY EXPENSES?

To figure out your monthly shortfall, or reduction amount, add up your total net income (your income after taxes are taken out) and enter it on line 1. Total your monthly expenses and enter it on line 2.

Line 1. Total Monthly Net Income $_____

Line 2. Subtract Your Total Monthly Expenses -$_____

Total Monthly Shortfall -$_____

This is the amount you need to reduce your monthly expenses: _____

The next step is to eliminate the shortfall (or difference) between what you make and what you spend. You now have the opportunity to decide which expenses you can cut out or reduce. Read Chapter

3, "Reducing Your Expenses", to figure out where you can cut down on spending.

Then, go back through all your expenditures for the month and see where you can reduce some of them by at least half, maybe eliminate others entirely. It's up to you to decide what to replace or reduce; this is where you can get creative in your budgeting plans.

REDUCING THOSE MONTHLY EXPENDITURES

List the reductions, remembering the goal is to reduce those monthly bills down to the amount you actually bring in per month.

Total Amount to Reduce $_____

EXPENSE	$ AMOUNT OF REDUCTION

TOTAL AMOUNT OF REDUCTIONS $ _____

Bank Reconciliations

It is critical to be familiar with all the expenditures going out of your bank account, to know which checks or payments are still outstanding, and to understand where your money is going every month.

HOW TO BALANCE YOUR BANK ACCOUNT

Start with your checkbook register. Mark off all the checks that the bank statement shows were cashed and ATM withdrawals shown on the statement. Next, make a list of the date and check number of any checks that were not cashed and ATM withdrawals not on your bank statement. These are known as outstanding checks or withdrawals:

Date   Check #   Check or Withdrawal Amount

_____

_____

_____

_____

_____

_____

_____

_____

Total of Oustanding Checks/Withdrawals $ _____

Get your checkbook balance by underlining the last transaction in your checkbook that includes cashed checks or ATM withdrawals.

List the balance in your account at the end $_____
of the statement period

Subtract any service charges made to your   -_____
account

Add any interest earned   +_____

This is your new check register balance $_____

From your account statement, list the $_____
statement ending balance

Add deposits shown in your check register   +_____
that aren't listed on your statement (known
as deposits in transit)

Subtract Total of Outstanding Checks/   -_____
Withdrawals, listed above

Balance should match the check register $_____
balance listed above

Chapter 3
Reducing Your Expenses

House or rent payments

Consider renting out a room in your house or apartment to cover part of the mortgage or rent payment. If you live in an apartment, make sure that subletting is allowed by your current rental agreement.

Some people may not consider this an option, but if you have several empty bedrooms and think you can handle roommates, this can earn you a significant amount of additional money.

Automobile expenses

CAR INSURANCE

1. Save on car insurance by comparing insurance rates online with various companies, making sure you check that each insurance plan has the features and coverage you need. When you find a less expensive insurance, switch to the new company.

GASOLINE EXPENSE

1. Use Google or any other search engine to check for the cheapest gas in your area. This can change on a daily or weekly basis so make sure you check for the least expensive gas each time you go to fill up.

2. Use your cruise control; this will save you on gas usage because more gas is expended when you continually accelerate and brake, especially on surface streets.

3. Don't go over the speed limit. According to the US Department of Energy, "gas mileage usually decreases rapidly at speeds above 50 mph. You can assume that each 5 mph you drive over 50 mph is like paying an additional $0.26 per gallon for gas. Observing the speed limit is also safer."[1]

   This will also save you big bucks because you won't be getting speeding tickets (if you do now), which can cost up to $400 and increase your auto insurance rates.

4. Get regular tune-ups for your car; this makes your engine more efficient. The more efficiently your car runs, the less gas it uses. "Fixing a car that is noticeably out of tune or has failed an emissions test can improve its gas mileage by an average of 4%."[2]

5. Empty your trunk! "Avoid keeping unnecessary items in your vehicle, especially heavy ones. An extra 100 pounds in your vehicle could reduce your mpg by up to 2%."[3]

6. Avoid excessive idling. Idling gets 0 miles per gallon. Cars with larger engines typically waste more gas at idle than cars with smaller engines.[4]

7. Use overdrive gears. "When you use overdrive gearing, your car's engine speed goes down." This can save gasoline and reduces engine wear.[5]

8. Maintaining your vehicle is inexpensive compared to a major breakdown. Proper maintenance will also save the exorbitant costs of renting a car while yours is in the shop. "Fixing a serious maintenance problem, such as a faulty oxygen sensor, can improve your mileage by as much as 40%."[6]

9. "Keep tires properly inflated. You can improve your gas mileage by up to 3.3% by keeping your tires inflated to the proper pressure. Underinflated tires can lower gas mileage by 0.3% for every 1 pound per square inch drop in pressure of all four tires. Properly inflated tires are safer and last longer."[7]

10. "Use the recommended grade of motor oil. You can improve your gas mileage by 1–2% by using the manufacturer's recommended grade of motor oil." "Also, look for motor oil that says 'Energy Conserving' on the API performance symbol to be sure it contains friction-reducing additives."[8]

CAR PAYMENTS

1. If you find that your car payment is more than one quarter of your monthly income, you should trade in your car for a less expensive automobile. You can also renegotiate your car loan to reduce the interest rate, saving the amount of money will you pay over the life of the loan.

2. Consider leasing a car, instead of buying one. The payments are usually lower, the leasing company may pay for some maintenance on the vehicle, and you get to drive around in a new car every three or four years!

<u>Saving on Utilities</u>

WATER

Eight Ways to Reduce Water Wasted on Your Yard

A study by the Pasadena Department of Water and Power determined that residential customers use approximately 112 gallons per day per person, much of which is used ineffectively by wasteful outdoor watering methods.

1. Did you know you can save up to 20 gallons per leak per day of wasted water by fixing leaks in your sprinkler system, by replacing broken heads or leaking connections?

2. Adjust outdoor sprinkler systems so they don't spray on sidewalks and patios; this will help eliminate up to 25 gallons per minute of wasted water. Don't allow runoff from landscape watering, as this clogs the gutter and pollutes the oceans. Water going into the sewers and storm drains isn't filtered; it runs straight to the ocean, causing serious pollution to coastal waters.

3. Remember to install a water recycling system if your home or business maintains decorative fountains or ponds.

4. Garden and landscape watering should be done before 10:00 a.m. and after 5:00 p.m. This way, less water will be wasted through evaporation. This can save up to 25 gallons of water usage per day.

5. Install a "smart" irrigation controller that automatically waters your outdoor plants based on weather conditions and soil moisture, or install a simple timer so you can keep outdoor watering down to once every 3–4 days.

6. Mulching around trees and plants can save up to 30 gallons of water per day, because the mulch helps the earth to retain water, and you lose less through evaporation.

7. You can install a catch-water system on your rooftop. Catch-water systems collect overnight moisture from the roof and funnel it into a basin, then after basic filtering it can be used to water your yard and garden.

8. Get creative in your garden, using indigenous, drought-resistant plants, or use rock or ornamental sand gardens.

Ten Ways to Reduce Water Wasted in Your Home

As much as 29 percent of residential water wastage could be eliminated by using these methods to reduce water wastage in your home. With a minimum of investment, you can save yourself money on your water bill, plus help your city through a serious drought.

1. Reduce your water pressure and you'll use less water when you turn on the faucet or shower.

2. Buy a five-minute water timer for your shower and get the family to take five-minute showers.

3. Use a bucket to catch excess water while you're taking a shower, and use that water in your plants or to flush the toilet.

4. Use a pitcher in the sink to save all the cold water that comes out while you're waiting for it to turn hot. You can reuse the water for rinsing dishes, watering plants, or flushing the toilet.

5. Save up to 20 gallons per leak per day of wasted water by fixing leaks in your home, by replacing broken showerheads or leaking connections.

6. Unbelievable as it may seem, if you turn off the water while brushing your teeth, you can save up to two gallons per minute of clean water from simply rushing down the drain.

7. By washing full loads of laundry instead of smaller loads, you can save up to 50 gallons per load.

8. Replace your inefficient older-model toilets with low-flow or high-efficiency toilets that save up to 3.8 gallons per flush.

9. Many city utility companies now offer rebates on buying and installing newer appliances, like high-efficiency clothes washers, ultra-low-water urinals, high-efficiency toilets, and smart irrigation controllers, so you not only conserve water but are saving money as well.

10. Use a low-flow showerhead to reduce water usage.

CLOTHES DRYER

1. Clean the filters in your dryer after every load, reducing the amount of time it will take to dry your clothes. This saves on your electricity or gas bill, depending on the type of energy used to dry your clothes.

2. When possible, air-dry your clothes outside.

HEATING WATER

1. Switch to all cold water for washing clothes; many laundry detergents are now made for use in cold water only. This will save on the money you spend unnecessarily heating the water.

2. The next time you need to replace your old-style water-heating tank, consider using a tankless water heater, which offers hot water on demand rather than continually heating 100 gallons of water (or more) at a time.

ELECTRICITY

1. Instead of leaving your outside lights on all night, replace them with outdoor lights with motion detectors. This way the lights will only go on if there is movement in your yard, which will also frighten off would-be burglars.

2. Use power strips for all your electrical appliances, and turn off the power strips at night (saving you eight hours of electrical usage), and while the family is at work or school (saving you another eight hours of electrical usage). Be aware of the ghost loads of electrical usage in your home. "Ghost load" refers to the electricity used by appliances that run even when you don't have them turned on, like ones that display the time.

3. Install solar panels on your home in order to produce your own electrical power, using Power Purchase Agreements (PPAs) or a leased system, which will allow you to install the panels free of cost and use the solar power for a small monthly fee.

4. Be conscious of utility bills; turn off lights and appliances when not in use.

5. Reduce your electric bill by replacing your old incandescent lighting with CFL (compact fluorescent lighting) or LED (light-emitting diode) lights. This can save you up to 30% on your lighting bill.

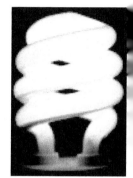

TRASH

Recycle as much household waste as you can, reducing the amount of trash you throw out. Some cities provide smaller trash bins and charge a lower rate to households that throw away less trash.

RECYCLING

Did you know that—in some cities—you can recycle: household metal (emptied canned food cans), household glass (anything that comes in a bottle or jar), paper (computer paper, recycled paper, newspaper, paper bags, junk mail), Styrofoam containers, plastic bottles (from toiletries, food, etc.) and plastic bags.
If you need to know if your city recycles certain items, call them and check before you put it in the recycling bin.

COMPOSTING

Raw food scraps—like carrot tops, potato peels, fruit peels, eggshells, the ends of lettuce or inedible lettuce leaves—can go into a compost pile, which will create good soil you can use in your garden and will keep that food out of the garbage disposal and out of your trash.

LARGE APPLIANCES

Comparison shopping:

1. Shop by telephone for the best purchase price on your big money items: appliances, electronic goodies, cars, etc. Talk it up among your coworkers and friends, if you plan to buy an expensive item. People like to share their horror stories and their successes alike, and you may get some good tips on where to go and where not to go for your particular item. Magazines like Consumer Reports make it their business to test and compare hundreds of products every year for quality and price. Take a quick trip to the library and locate the issue you need to look up the information on the product you plan to buy.

2. Play the competition against each other. Remember, the salesperson wants to sell the item to you as much as you want to buy it, so quote their competitor's price and don't be afraid to try to get them to lower their price. Sometimes this ploy works, but sometimes the price can't be changed by the salesperson. If you think you have some bargaining power, you can ask to speak to a manager in charge who may have the ability to lower the price.

EATING OUT

When you feel like eating out, treat yourself to breakfast instead of dinner. It's the cheapest meal of the day. At some fast-food restaurants, you may not have to tip, saving you 15% of the meal's cost. Take the extra food home so you have part of your next meal prepared.

Sign up for the restaurant's email list to receive coupons, find out when they have specials, or be alerted to their "kids eat free" dining times/days.

GROCERIES

Don't pay full price for anything! Many stores and supermarkets sell name-brand food and toiletries for half price if you buy in bulk. It's worth the savings to clean out a hall closet and use it for the storage of extra paper products and dry goods, in order to buy larger amounts. For example: Costco, Smart & Final, Sam's Club and other discount store prices are usually half what you pay in the grocery stores. While you can't get everything you need from the clubs, you can get a lot of name-brand products for huge savings off your food bill.

Make sure to make a list when you go grocery shopping; this will cut down on impulse buying. When using coupons, make a notation on your list of the brand name and number of items you need to buy to receive your discount. Tape the coupons to your list so you won't have to dig through your purse and shuffle through your coupons to find the ones you'll end up using on this trip.

<u>Use Coupons for Everything!</u>

You can save lots of money by shopping with coupons. You will find you can save money on groceries, dining out, entertainment, clothing; in fact, you can save on just about anything you regularly buy.

If you think clipping coupons is a hassle and a huge waste of time, consider using online coupons. Here are some examples of ways to save using online coupons.

EATING OUT

Earn free meals from your favorite restaurants when you sign on to receive their email offers. You can receive at least two to three coupons a month offering a free drink, free dessert, or "buy one meal, get one meal half-off" via the Internet. Many restaurants offer a rewards program: When you go to eat at the restaurant you swipe a rewards card. When you accrue a certain number of points, you earn food rewards.

GIFT GIVING

Earn rewards for reading short emails from www.mypoints.com. When you sign up for this service they send you emails from their sponsor companies, which you can read in a few seconds, earning you rewards points. One Christmas when I was low on money, I redeemed points I had earned for gift cards and gave all the adults in my family gift cards for their favorite stores. They had a ball shopping for clothes, shoes and books at the stores they like the most, and they got exactly what they wanted for Christmas.

TOILETRIES

Find an online coupon service for your favorite products; for example, www.bucksbee.com offers you coupons for 10 to 20% off your favorite brands of laundry soap, cleaning products, and toiletries. Or Google the name of the products you use and join their online website.

GROCERIES

Sign up for your local market's club card; you'll save money on groceries, and everything else you buy at the market. You can go online and sign up with your local market to have your coupons downloaded onto your club card from the computer. For example, Ralph's market has an option on their website to choose the coupons you want to

use and download them onto your rewards card electronically. This way, you don't have to cut them out, organize them or carry them around. Check out the website at www.ralphs.com.

ENTERTAINMENT

The Entertainment Coupon Book (www.entertainment.com) offers coupons for movies, local sporting events, other entertainment venues, restaurants and fast food, clothing and gifts. Wait until April to buy the book, when the prices are lowest.

OFFICE SUPPLIES

Sign on to OfficeMax to receive coupons for office supplies.

Savings on Insurances

HEALTH INSURANCE

Many people have health insurance through work, but if you are stuck paying the high rates for health insurance, consider shopping around for less expensive insurance well before the renewal date. Read all the information on coverage for the procedures and type of health care your family needs, and make sure you understand the deductibles, co-pays and coinsurance so you'll know exactly which portion of the costs you'll be responsible for.

The Children's Health Insurance Program (CHIP) provides subsidized health insurance coverage to children of families who don't qualify for Medicaid but cannot afford private health insurance. Find out about the program at their website http://www. chipmedicaid.org.

DENTAL INSURANCE

These tips might help you save on dental insurance (if you don't already have it through your employer):

1. Ask the office manager if you can arrange a payment plan so you can make monthly payments instead of paying the whole bill at once.

2. If you have a major procedure done, arrange to have your treatments several months apart so you can spread the payments out.

3. If you don't have employer-provided dental insurance, research

your own dental plan through providers like www.dentalplans.com, www.brighter.com, or the AARP (American Association of Retired People) dental network at http://www.aarp.org.

4. For routine dental cleanings, check out if there are dental schools in your area. The students get hands-on experience and are supervised by licensed dentists, and you get dental care for as much as one-third off the regular price.

Smoking, Your Health and Your Budget

Cigarettes can be a big drain on your health and on your budget. At this writing, cigarettes cost approximately $5.00 per pack, and the next ballot will bring up the possibility of voters increasing the taxes on cigarettes an additional $1.07 per pack, which would bring the total to a whopping $6.07 per pack. That's a huge chunk of a smoker's monthly budget.

Health-related problems caused by smoking include cancer of the lungs, mouth, larynx and lips, can cost millions of dollars to treat, and can eventually cost you your life.

There are state-funded smoking cessation classes (in California, go to www.ccfc.ca.gov and click on Tobacco Cessation), or call the California Smokers' Helpline at 1-800-NO-BUTTS. If you live outside of California, search the internet for classes and help lines in your area.

As an alternative to quitting cold turkey, consider smoking the new "smokeless" cigarettes to help you break the habit.

Ten Tips on Living Frugally to Reduce Your Expenses

1. Cancel all unnecessary periodicals, magazines and newspapers.

2. Become aware of your shopping habits; evaluate any nonessential spending.

3. Barter your services for services you need; use a short one-page contract that specifies what services you will give for the services you will receive.

4. Instead of buying flowers for gifts, trim flowers from your yard and arrange them in a secondhand glass vase for a quick birthday present or for any other occasion. This will save you money and give your gift a more personal touch.

5. Recycling can save you money! Instead of buying wrapping paper for gifts, you can reuse the beautiful calendar pages from last year's calendar, or use the colorful comic section from your newspaper for children's gifts.

6. Instead of buying expensive art to decorate your work space, use free posters from travel agencies. What better scenery to look at on your work break than a lovely vacation spot?

7. Save and reuse fabric softener sheets to clean out the dryer lint filter after every load (and cleaning out the filter will extend the life of your dryer). The used sheets can also be used to dust furniture, instead of using expensive duster sheets.

8. Instead of throwing away a tube of toothpaste before you've used it all, invest in some inexpensive toothpaste squeezers to help you squeeze the last bit out of the tube.

9. Most liquid laundry detergent is highly concentrated, so once you've used about ¼ of the product, start adding a capful of clean water to the container with every wash to make that soap last longer. Also, the inside of the container usually has a thick residue of soap inside it, so make sure to fill the empty bottle halfway full of water, shake it up and watch how much longer you can make the soap last.

10. Make a grocery list before you go to the store; tell your family, "If it's not on the list, it's not coming home!" This will save you trips back to the store in the middle of the week and help to cut down on impulse buying while you shop.

How to Celebrate the Holidays for Less

MOTHER'S DAY, FATHER'S DAY

Homemade is still the best! Consider making your mom/dad a gift, whether from the garden, your kitchen or your craft table. Making a gift with your own hands says "I love you" with your personal touch. In today's hustle-bustle world, taking the time to create your own card and gift tells the recipient you are thinking of them while you create their gift. Sometimes just spending time with people is all they really want, so consider taking the time to spend an afternoon or evening with your mom or dad for Mother's Day or Father's Day.

If you decide you'd like to take Mom/Dad out to a meal, the restaurant will probably be packed, so if you want to avoid crowds, taking them the Saturday before the holiday can be more pleasant and less expensive. Combining those holidays is also a nifty way to get a two-for-one!

Chapter 4
Eliminating Credit Card Debt

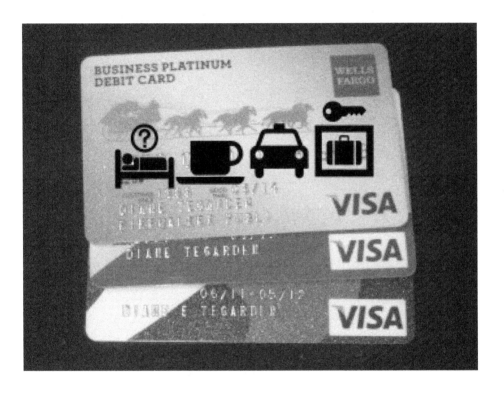

Eliminating Credit Card Debt

This is a method I have used to eliminate my credit card debt, and since then, I've shared it with many, many people. Using this method, many of them have managed to dig themselves out of credit card debt in three years or less. This may seem like a long time, but many people, if left to their own financial devices, end up in deeper debt or bankruptcy within that time.

1. **Make a list of all your credit cards,** using columns for each of these items: name of credit card, interest rate on the card, and the total amount due.

Name of Credit Card	Interest Rate	Total Amount Due

2. **Figure out how much you pay** in total in credit card payments per month.

3. **Find the credit card you are closest to paying off with the highest interest rate.** It is very important to understand that when you are buying items on credit you are paying more for them than the actual "sales" price; this is how the credit card companies make their money. Therefore, if you pay off this card first, you are automatically saving money by not paying a higher interest rate on the temporary loans we call credit card debt.

4. It is critical to take this next step, even if it is extremely painful. While paying off a credit card, you must **cut up the card and not use the account again**. Make a ceremony of it—take a big pair of scissors, and while cackling with glee, snip that debt into little unrecognizable pieces. It's exhilarating; try it, try it, I say!!

Interest Rates and Annual Membership Fees

When choosing a credit card, the percentage of interest is more important than other perks, for example, getting cash back for your purchases or rewards points. Make sure the interest rate is low and fixed at that rate, or it's not a good deal. Also, check to see if you will have to pay a yearly membership fee; not paying a membership fee can save you up to $150 a year.

Learn How to Do the Credit Card Shuffle

In the credit card shuffle, you take advantage of those wonderful special offers you're always receiving in the mail. Namely, a special offer for a credit card with a really low Annual Percentage Rate

(APR) of 3% or less, for a limited time only, usually six months. Fill out the application, and when they ask you about credit card transfers, transfer the total amount you usually pay per month on higher-rate credit cards, multiplied by the number of months the special rate is in effect. Transfer only this amount from the higher-interest-rate card to the new card. Make sure to pay it off completely within that time period, because after that the rates go up.

After you have paid off the card, cancel the card formally in writing, and keep a copy of your cancellation letter for yourself. In order to clean up your credit report and earn better interest rates and higher credit limits in the future, you must first get those outstanding debts off your record by paying them off. Then, once you actually cancel your account, your financial picture looks better to bankers and other people checking your credit.

One more note, that may surprise you, about the money shuffle. You may think, "It won't impress anyone to get a credit card and cancel it in six months." Oh, how wrong you are, my friend. In fact, paying off a debt on time is so very impressive that after you do this just once, more credit card companies will come calling at your door.

And I encourage you to avail yourself of another opportunity to play the money shuffle, to keep transferring your debts from a higher-interest card to the lower one, eliminating the largest debt and establishing a new credit profile. I suggest you immediately cut up all the clothing-store credit cards and specialty-store credit cards. These usually have higher interest rates than other cards, so this method of deciding which credit cards to use can save you hundreds of dollars a year in disposable debts.

What is your credit rating?

First of all, to find out what your credit rating is, call go online to www.AnnualCreditReport.com and get your annual free credit report. It's the only legitimate FREE website where you can obtain your credit report. All you have to do is give them your name, address, date of birth and social security number, and you can get a record of your borrowing and bill payment history. If you'd rather fill out a paper claim, write to:

Annual Credit Report Request Service
P.O. Box 105283, Atlanta, GA 30348-5283

Your credit rating can affect your ability to qualify for home loans, car loans—even affect your ability to get your next job. Having a good credit rating means you may qualify for a 0% interest rate on car loans, may get a loan on your home at a lower interest rate and may even qualify for that dream job you've always wanted, so it's important to make sure your credit rating is as high as you can make it.

Improving Your Credit Rating

By law, the following agencies are allowed to access your credit report: employers who are considering you for a job; lenders who are considering issuing you a loan on your home, for an auto or for a credit card; insurers who are considering issuing you auto insurance; and government agencies. That is why it's so important to know your credit rating and to keep your record complete and accurate.

If there are any discrepancies or errors on the report, get in touch with the lender that reported the error, and ask them how you can get the information corrected.

These are the three major credit-reporting agencies:

1. **Experian,** P.O. Box 9556, Allen, TX 75013-9556
888-397-3742
www.experian.com

2. **Equifax,** P.O. Box 740241, Atlanta, GA 30374-0241
800-685-1111
www.equifax.com

3. **TransUnion,** P.O. Box 2000, Chester, PA 19022-2000
800-916-8800
www.transunion.com

(All contact information was current at the time of publication.)

To learn more about contacting credit bureaus, you can go to http://www.bankrate.com/finance/credit-debt/contacting-the-credit-bureaus.aspx#ixzz1ssb1YbSS.

THE FEDERAL TRADE COMMISSION

You can also contact the Federal Trade Commission (FTC), a government agency that works to prevent fraudulent, deceptive and unfair business practices in the marketplace. The FTC also teaches consumers how to spot, stop and avoid fraudulent, deceptive and unfair business practices. To file a complaint or get free information on consumer issues, visit www.ftc.gov or call toll-free: 877-382-4357. For an instructive video on how to file a complaint, see ftc.gov/video.

MORE CONSUMER PROTECTION AGENCIES

Two more consumer groups you can check out are the Consumer Financial Protection Bureau (at www.consumerfinance.gov or call toll-free at 855-411-2372), which was created to protect consumers from aggressive collection agencies, and the Office for Older Americans (at http://www.consumerfinance.gov/older-americans), a group designed to protect senior citizens from elder financial abuse and telemarketer schemes.

REPORT STOLEN CREDIT OR DEBIT CARDS RIGHT AWAY!

If your credit card is stolen, federal law requires you to pay the first $50.00 of the debt, but most credit card companies will waive this if you report it right away and can prove the credit card or number was stolen.

However, if your debit card is stolen, you are liable for up to:

- $50.00 if the loss is reported within two business days,
- $500.00 if the loss is reported after two business days,
- the total amount if the loss is reported after 60 days.

So, remember to check your wallet every few days to make sure you still have all your debit and credit cards.

Two more great reasons to keep your credit rating squeaky clean:

1. You may get a better job because of your high credit scores.

2. You can qualify for lower interest rates on your mortgage and car loans.

Chapter 5
Save Your Money!

How to Start Saving Money

1. **You can start a savings account by using the "Keep the Change" program at Bank of America;** the program automatically transfers small amounts of money to your savings account when you use your debit card. For example, let's say you charge $12.85 to your debit card. Bank of America rounds that amount up to the nearest whole dollar amount ($13.00) and deposits $.15 into your savings account. This doesn't sound like much, but let's say the total amount they transfer to your savings account is approximately $7.85 per month: You will have already saved $94.20 in one year. Additionally, Bank of America will match the savings for the first three months you're in the program. Hey! That means you're getting free money from the bank!

2. **Set up an automatic transfer from your checking account to your savings account.** Have your bank automatically transfer $20 per week from your checking to your savings account and in one year you will have saved $1040.00. Only use this account for the emergencies that inevitably come up when you have a growing family, whether medical emergency, car repair or breakdown of one of your major appliances.

3. **Set up direct deposit for your paycheck to be deposited into your checking account.** This will help you pay your bills on time every month, especially if you have automatic payments coming out of your checking account.

4. **Join a credit union.** This is especially useful when you need to borrow money at a lower rate and save at a higher rate than at a bank!

5. Instead of borrowing from credit cards with high interest rates, **consider borrowing money from your life insurance policy**

in the event of an emergency. **This will save you the higher interest rates you pay on credit cards.**

6. **Pay your bills on time to avoid late fees and high finance charges.** It may seem like an oversimplification, but if you pay your bills on time, you will avoid late fees and higher interest charges, and your credit rating will improve.

PAYING ON TIME CAN BE DONE IN SEVERAL WAYS

1. The first way is to pay your bill as soon as you receive it. This will put your mind at rest that your bills are paid on time, whether by check or online. By printing out a copy of your payment you have a paper trail to prove your bill was paid on time.

2. Let's say you get paid twice a month. Here's a way to set up a very simple filing system, consisting of a letter-size cardboard box, two hanging files and four file folders.

   Label one hanging file with a tag that reads JAN/MAR/MAY/JULY/SEPT/NOV. Label the other file with a tag that reads FEB/APR/JUNE/AUG/OCT/DEC.

   (The reason you only need two hanging files is that most bills will be due in the month you receive them, or in the following month.)

   Next, mark the top of two file folders with "Pay on the 15th"; the other two folders will be marked "Pay on the 30th". Get a letter-size cardboard box and put one folder marked with 15th and one folder marked with 30th into each hanging folder.

   When a bill comes in, check to see when the bill is due, and put it in the correct folder so you can pay it in time. For example, if a bill is due on the 1st–15th of April, put it in the file folder marked "Pay on the 30th" in the hanging file that has MAR (March) on the tag (keeping in mind that the bills due exactly on the 1st should be paid a few days ahead of time to take mailing time into consideration). If a bill is due on the 16th–30th of April, put it in the file folder marked "Pay on the 15th" in the APR hanging file (keeping in mind that the bills due exactly on the 16th should be paid a few days ahead of time to take mailing time into consideration).

Then, every payday, pay the bills in the appropriate folder, and you'll never pay them late!

3. Paying online by automatic payments. Some banks offer free online bill pay, and with some accounts you can set up an automatic bill payment for recurring payments. Just remember to record those payments in your check register, so your record is up to date.

   A good reason to pay your bills online is that you are constantly monitoring your account. If there are any suspicious charges, you can catch them and challenge them right away. By paying online you can save up to $60.00 per year in stamps, save the time you would have spent writing out checks and driving to the post office, and save on those nasty late fees.

ANOTHER GOOD REASON TO PAY YOUR BILLS ON TIME

If you usually pay your bills on time and occasionally make a mistake and pay late, call the company you make the payments to and ask for the billing department. Patiently and politely ask the billing clerk to check on your account to see that you usually pay on time. Explain that you made a mistake this month and paid late, and you'd like to have the late fee reversed, if possible. Most of the time, if you have a good payment record and are a longtime customer in good standing, they'll reverse the charges. They'll only do this occasionally, so don't rely on it if you usually pay late.

Thinking Frugally Can Save You Money

How you spend your money is your business. Many people feel "poor" no matter how much money they have or spend, so your attitude toward spending and saving is as important as how much money you make.

For example, if I were to ask you "if a person makes five million dollars a year, is that a lot of money?" Most people would automatically answer with a resounding "YES!"

But my next question would be "how much does that person spend?" If the person spends ten million, then actually, five million dollars is NOT a lot of money!

So you have to ask yourself, how can I live on the amount of money I make NOW? If you spend money to make yourself feel better after your feelings have been hurt, then you are using money as an emotional Band-Aid. Emotional spending doesn't actually make you feel better; at least, the good feelings don't last, and consequently, you have to go back and spend more. So, the next time you're about to go on a spending binge, ask yourself "do I need this item, or do I want it to make myself feel better for the moment?"

Usually, you can figure out a better, more lasting way to make yourself happy than by buying stuff you don't really need.

Let's take a popular example of overspending that may be an eye-opener for some of you.

Lots of people go out for expensive coffee drinks every morning on the way to work. This costs you money, time and gas on the trip, plus the coffee is usually loaded with sugar and cream, meaning lots of extra calories you probably don't need.

You may say "I can't live without my fancy coffee in the mornings." Fine. Don't give up your java habit, but you can save an incredible amount of money by buying an espresso machine/coffeemaker for your home.

Let's do the math. Say your coffee habit costs $3.60 per day at Joe Shmoe's Coffee Emporium. Assuming you only drink one cup per workday, that's
$3.60 x 5 days a week = $18.00 per week x 52 weeks per year = a whopping $936.00 per year!

If you were to buy a fancy espresso machine for $336.00, you'd save $600.00 the first year you use the machine and $936.00 every year after that (minus the cost of coffee, sugar, cream, and flavorings) using your own coffee machine! And that's a lot of money.

Chapter 6
Keeping Track Of Your Money

Track Your Money

1. Recurring payments.

For bills that are the same exact amount every month, it's hard to keep track if you miss a payment or the bank hasn't received a payment because it's the same exact dollar amount. When paying recurring payments of the same exact amount, use the decimal place to indicate the month you're making the payment.

For example, let's say you have a payment that's $57.00 per month. In January, pay $57.01; in February pay $57.02, etc. This way, if there is a question about a missing payment, you can ask the bank which payments they have received and you can figure out which payment has been misplaced.

Each month your balance will be credited with the extra payment, and by December, your bill will have a credit of $.66. This means your last payment in December should be $56.34, which will clear out your payments due for the year. This will bring the payments back to an even $57.00 in January, and you always know which payments your bank has received and which ones are lost in the mail.

2. Paying property taxes.

Property taxes can be tricky because the bill only comes once a year, with vouchers to pay it in two payments. So you're hit with two huge payments you have to come up with seemingly out of the blue. In order to avoid the horrible surprise of paying this huge amount twice a year, divide the total bill by 12; this is the monthly amount you should be transferring to a savings account. Set up your checking account to transfer the monthly balance in two easy payments per month, let's say on your paydays (if you are paid twice a month). This way, instead of having to borrow from your credit cards to pay your property taxes, you'll have that money safely tucked away in your savings account.

3. Face tax time with assurance.

If you end up with a huge personal tax bill at the end of the year, instead of waiting until tax time with dread, arrange a small weekly transfer to your savings account that will cover the bill. For example: Say you usually owe $4000 in taxes at the end of the year. If you transfer just $77 per week to a savings account, instead of freaking out next March, you'll have the money in the bank.

4. A way to avoid owing taxes at the end of the year.

When you apply for a job, instead of taking the usual number of deductions on your W4, choose zero. Yes, zero! Your employer will deduct a little more than you actually owe out of your paycheck for payroll taxes each pay period. At the end of the year, the government will owe you money and not the other way around!

Some people will argue the point; they'll claim that this way you are letting the government make interest on the extra money they're holding. I would argue that the money the government earns is very small. Besides, most people will spend that money as soon as they are paid, so that money just disappears. Whereas if the government is holding it for you, you'll get it back in one lump sum at tax time, rather than spending it as you go.

The other objection is you "could be putting that extra money in a savings account and earning interest on it." Again, my experience while counseling people about their finances tells me that they probably won't put the money in a savings account; they'll spend it as soon as they get it. Even if you did put it in a savings account, the small amount of interest you'll earn won't be worth the value you'll get when you receive one huge tax refund at tax time and then put that money in an interest-bearing CD (certificate of deposit).

5. Keep a file for your end-of-year paperwork (for tax time).

You'll need one cardboard box, a few hanging files, and file folders. Keep all the receipts from donations, home improvements, IRA (individual retirement account) contributions, and money you spend on a tax preparer.

If you have a home based business, keep all receipts for business expenses, utility bills (you will be able to deduct a percentage of your bills, based on the square footage of the room where you conduct your business), and rent or mortgage payments.

6. Keep track of your household expenses.

To track your household expenses, consider buying an accounting program such as QuickBooks (QB) or Quicken. This may take some time to set up initially, but you'll be able to figure out exactly how much you spend in each area of your finances, which will help you see where you can cut down on some of those out-of-control bills.

Chapter 7
Busting Some Big Budget Myths

Budget Myth #1: Christmas Gifts

Warning: This subject may be considered controversial! Quit guilt holiday shopping. Christmas gifts bring on big debts and big guilt. Christmas is supposed to be a blessed time of year, but it often turns into a recurring financial nightmare for many families.

12 WAYS TO AVOID THE CHRISTMAS CRUNCH

1. Instead of giving individual presents, which can set you back hundreds of dollars (depending on the size of your extended family), have a family party. Each family brings a food dish, a specialty Christmas food they enjoy making, and swaps recipes. Everyone can bring a favorite food dish, or sweets, and share their funny and harrowing stories from the year gone past. Instead of presents, adults might give each other IOUs for favors like babysitting, gardening, a massage or a facial, or to share whatever their special hidden talents may be.

2. Have the kids create short Christmas plays to entertain everyone. Help the children present a play to the rest of the family; each child could share a tale of the past year's adventures or a family anecdote that brings you together. This is the time of year to share a part of your life your family may have missed or just to catch up on the latest family news.

3. Copy the lyrics to Christmas carols and have a sing-along.

4. Before Christmas, have a lottery where all the families put each family member's name in a bowl and each member of the family draws the name of one person they will buy a gift for. This reduces the number of gifts each family has to buy. Set a dollar limit on the gifts and make everyone stick to the limit!

5. For friends and coworkers, give gifts of homemade food (jam, cookies, brownies, etc.) in an attractive basket. My specialty is homemade cranberry sauce (killer good!).

6. Use gift bags instead of wrapping paper to save on the expense of wrapping paper that will just end up in the trash. If you receive gifts in gift bags, save and reuse them for next year.

7. Save at least $10.00 to spend after Christmas for seriously marked-down wrapping paper, gift cards and Christmas cards (if you still choose to use these items next Christmas).

8. Send free electronic cards to all the people on your list who have email; it's much cheaper than Christmas cards and saves loads of time. Some websites with free ecards: www.jibjab.com, www.myfuncards.com, www.americangreetings.com, www. punchbowl.com.

9. Regifting is ok; just make sure you write down who gave you the gift on a Post-it note so you don't give it back to the same person who gave it to you!

10. Starting in the New Year, plan to buy one or two gifts each month for the people on your Christmas list. This way you're not hit with a huge bill at the end of each year.

11. For those people who have everything, or always manage to buy themselves everything they need, consider donating a small amount to their favorite charity. Most charities will send a nice Christmas card to the recipient with your name on it, letting them know a gift has been given to the charity, in their name.

12. Start a modest Christmas savings account and only use cash or checks to pay for Christmas next year. DO NOT succumb to credit card debt for Christmas giving.

My #1 rule of Christmas finance:
If you are still paying off last year's credit card debts due to Christmas shopping by the time next Christmas rolls around, you are overspending!

Budget Myth #2: New Clothes

Why you don't need a new wardrobe every season

Beware the "new-clothes myth" that can ruin your budget. We know women are encouraged to be obsessed with their wardrobe, and expected to buy matching clothes, shoes and purses with each new fashion and season. This is a colossal waste of money!

1. Remember, in any budget, clothes are considered a disposable expense, because they can be used up in a year or less, while a well-maintained car is considered an invested expense because it can last up to ten years. (In some cases, part of the expense for your car can be written off your taxable income as a business expense. These are called employee reimbursable expenses—maintenance and gas, for example.)

2. If you think buying new clothing will get you a raise, just look around at the company where you work. Chances are, the people at the top have about five good suits that they wear week in and week out, not hundreds of items of new clothes to impress the lower ranks. Their work, their degrees, their experience and their buddies (who they know) earn them their raises. Knowing how to make that money work for them is what helps them keep their money in their bank account. Making less of your appearance, spending a sensible amount on clothes, makeup, bags, shoes and other accessories, makes your boss concentrate on your work, not your looks. This is how you will earn more.

3. If you must buy new clothing, make sure you can use it for several types of occasions, not just for work. And consider the money you will save, not to mention the environment, when you buy washable clothes instead of ones that need to be dry-cleaned!

4. Finally, if you have children, consider taking them to an upscale thirdhand store. It will be a funky adventure for them to choose their own wild outfits, saving you lots of money on clothes they will soon outgrow anyway. This will give the kids some individuality in their wardrobe without making them feel poverty-stricken.

Budget Myth #3: Buying in Bulk

Buying in bulk is ALWAYS best—NOT so!

For one thing, if the items are perishable food, like vegetables, fruit or milk products, and your family doesn't consume them, the rotten food represents money you wasted, not money you saved.

You can stock up on paper products, canned food, dried food, cleaning products and toiletries, if you have the room to store them. And, watch out for expiration dates on canned and dry food, because some items you think aren't perishable just may be.

Budget Myth #4: BOGO

Always take advantage of BOGO (Buy One–Get One Pair Half-Off): WRONG again!

There are only so many pairs of shoes you need, and if you get two pairs because one is half price, you are still paying more than if you only buy what you need.

Now, if you are going with a friend or family member who also needs new shoes, buy both pairs and split the cost, so you both get shoes for less.

Chapter 8
Increasing Your Income

Education is the Answer to a Higher Wage

One thing to consider is increasing your income by improving your saleable skills. If you attain a higher level of education, whether you get a certificate from a trade school, an Associate of Arts (AA) or Associate of Science (AS) degree from a two-year college, or a BA, MA or PhD from a university, you will instantly be worth more money in the job market.

The question then becomes "which school is right for you?"

Trade School
The advantage with trade schools is they offer the shortest time frame in which to complete the requirements to get your certificate, sometimes as little as 8–12 months. If your main concern is time, consider a trade school. Also, these schools usually have job placement.

Two-Year College
These courses take longer to complete, usually 3–4 years. If your main concern is cost, and you have limited resources available, consider this: You may qualify for some type of financial aid (available at all three types of schools). Also, two-year colleges are very inexpensive and geared for returning students.

Four-Year College
These degrees take the longest to complete. A "four-year degree" (bachelor degree) can actually take 4–8½ years to complete, considering the class offerings, changes in course requirements, or changes of major.

Which school/education level should you make your goal?
Consider what type of job you're looking for and the educational requirements of the position you want. The chart below provides

some examples but is not exhaustive. Note that some four-year-college jobs listed below require further education.

Trade Schools *Type of Job*	Two-Year College *Type of Job*	4-Year College *Type of Job*
Medical Assistant	LVN/RN	Doctor
Bookkeeper	Business Administrator	CPA
Dental Assistant		Dentist
Paralegal	Pre-Law	Lawyer
Sales Assistant	Sales Manager	
CADD/Drafter		Architect
Website Designer	System Adminstrator	
Computer Progammer	System Adminstrator	

I have graduated from both academic and trade schools, and I found advantages and disadvantages in each.

ADVANTAGES OF A TRADE SCHOOL

1. It takes a shorter period of time to complete the course work and to graduate or become certified.

2. There are various forms of financial assistance. Programs cost less for people at lower income levels.

3. They are usually more flexible about working around an employed adult's schedule.

4. Because trade schools offer a more limited curriculum than

academic schools, they usually focus more on the area of study the student is interested in, eliminating the problem of having to take classes of absolutely no interest to the student.

5. Many trade schools have a placement office to help graduates get good entry-level jobs right out of school.

The one serious limitation I've found to trade schools is that you earn a certificate, not a degree, so if you are looking to get a job that requires a degree, you should consider an academic institution.

ADVANTAGES OF COLLEGES AND UNIVERSITIES

Both junior colleges and universities are academic institutions that award various degrees, from associate to PhD. The main disadvantage of going to a university is that it takes a long time to go through a degree program, anywhere from 4 to 8½ years, depending on how many hours you have to work. However, the advantage is that you can now qualify for the higher-paying jobs that require a degree (see chart above).

A word of warning: Competition is fierce in the entry-level job market for people with a BA or BS. Make sure you get some on-the-job training in your chosen field before you graduate and go looking for a job. You'll be many steps ahead of the competition.

If you haven't been to school in over ten years and don't know where to start, consider attending a community college. They often have classes designed for working adults who want to retrain for another career. These classes are designed to prepare you for the higher-level college coursework.

LIST OF TRADE SCHOOLS IN THE US

Websites listing information on trade schools

Trade Schools Guide—find a great school
www.trade-schools.net

U.S. Department of Education Database of Accredited Trade Schools
www.ope.ed.gov/accreditation

Vocational Schools—business, trade and technical
www.rwm.org

Trade school websites

American Trade School— electrical, heating, air-conditioning, refrigeration
www.stltrades.com

Aviation College—aviation maintenance
www.crimsontech.edu

California Trade School—accounting, business, carpentry, computer tech, criminal justice, dental, electrician, HVAC, massage, medical assistant, medical billing, nursing, paralegal, pharmacy, plumbing
www.everest.edu

Health-Care Trade School—medical, dental, surgical assistant, optical, massage, respiratory, pharmacy, vocational nursing, medical billing, health information technology
http://www.americancareercollege.edu

ITT Tech—IT (Information Technology), computers and telecommunications
www.itt-tech.edu

Ivy Bridge College of Tiffin University—accounting, business, computer IT, corrections, health-care administration, criminal justice for homeland security, law enforcement, sports management
www.ivybridge.tiffin.edu

Lincoln Technical Institute—automotive, business management, collision repair, computer networking and security, cosmetology, criminal justice, culinary, dental, diesel, electrician, medical, nursing, paralegal, pharmacy, welding, x-ray technician
www.lincolntech-usa.com

Marinello Beauty Schools—beautician, manicurist
www.marinello.com

North American Trade School (in Maryland)—building construction technician, CDL training, diesel technician training, electrical technology, HVAC, combination welding technology, industrial maintenance training
www.natradeschools.com

North-West College—nursing, vocational nurse, pharmacy technician, medical insurance billing
www.north-westcollege.edu

The Refrigeration School —HVAC (heating, ventilation and air-conditioning)
www.refrigerationschoolinc.com/

SOCHI Massage School—massage therapy
www.sochi.edu

South Bay College—massage programs
www.southbaycollege.adzzoo.com

UEI College—medical assistant, dental assistant, IT, business
www.ueicollege.com

University of Phoenix® —technical courses and IT degrees
www.phoenix.edu/IT

Westwood College, L.A.—20 programs available in technology, business, health care, justice, design, automotive technology
www.westwood.edu/LosAngelesCA

WSI Designer Marketplace—interior designers, architects
www.wsidesignermarketplace.com

WYO Tech—automotive, diesel, collision/refinishing, motorcycle, marine, HVAC, plumbing, electrician
http://goto.wyotech.edu

Brainstorming Problems

In the next several pages, we will use some forms to set up your academic plan in steps.

Let us start by brainstorming the problem.

The first step in BRAINSTORMING a problem is writing down as many parts of the problem as you can think of. As fast as you can, write down all the obstacles that stand in your way. Don't worry about being neat; just jot down the different aspects of the problem you want to solve. At this phase, don't worry about prioritizing the different parts, and don't try to come up with solutions just yet. You will prioritize them in the next step. Write down anything that comes to mind, no matter how silly, trite or ridiculous. Then leave the list to sit overnight.

After you have left the list alone overnight, cross out the things that seem less important or less critical to solve right away. Reduce the list to the top ten obstacles.

Now, write down at least two possible solutions for each obstacle.

Use the Brainstorming Form on the next page to help you make your lists of obstacles and solutions.

BRAINSTORMING FORM FOR ACADEMIC ACHIEVEMENT

OBSTACLE	SOLUTION	SOLUTION
1.		
2.		
3.		
4.		
5.		
6.		
7.		
8.		
9.		
10.		

Chapter 9
Planning Your
Financial Freedom

Free Financial Information

Take advantage of the ways you can learn about finances without spending any money.

1. Your local community may offer free financial seminars that are taught by financial planners, attorneys, and accountants, to name a few. Go to as many of these as you like and take notes. Keep in mind you're there to learn, not to buy. If you are approached by anyone selling products or services, just say, "I enjoyed your seminar and learned a lot, but I'm not interested in buying at this time." Do not give out your name, address or phone number on mailing lists; this way you won't be solicited at a later time.

   At these seminars you will be surrounded by other people who are there to learn, and you may begin to establish new business contacts.

2. Another place to check for financial information is your local library or community center that offers similar programs. Do a computer search for local seminars in your area, and remember to take a notebook with you so you can retain all the relevant information.

3. There are several TV and internet shows dedicated to teaching you about your finances. Many will have episodes archived on various subjects and you can listen/watch one per week to absorb new information.

Financial education boils down to understanding the simple principles of addition and subtraction. You will be amazed at how everything can be broken down to pluses or minuses. What you earn is the plus side, what you spend is the minus side, it's up to you to learn what your numbers are, then to reduce your spending below what you earn.

Once you have mastered living within your means, the next step would be to increase your earnings

Using the Stepping Stones Flowchart

Once you have chosen your solutions to each financial obstacle, write them in doable steps for each quarter of the next year using the Stepping Stones Flowchart.

Looking at your progress every three months (or quarter) gives you more time to get some of the steps completed before you check where you are. This allows you to feel more of a sense of accomplishment than by checking your flowchart every month.

Remember to use the chart to see your progress and celebrate successes at every quarter ending. You don't have to be lavish—just take a moment to cross off the things you've done, and treat yourself to a quiet cup of congratulations.

Be flexible and realistic with your chart. Take into consideration the busier times of year and don't overschedule those months. Keep some space available for the longer steps and for the ones that will inevitably carry over into the next quarter.

The Stepping Stones Flowchart

First three months of your plan _____

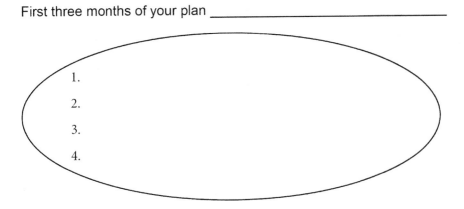

1.

2.

3.

4.

The Stepping Stones Flowchart *(continued)*

Next three months of your plan _____

1.

2.

3.

4.

Next three months of your plan _____

1.

2.

3.

4.

Final three months of your plan _____

1.

2.

3.

4.

Chapter 10
Retirement Planning

Considerations for Retirement Planning

While it's true many negative factors affect retirement planning for the vast majority of people, there is still hope. Your basic retirement budget should take into consideration your monthly income, expenses, savings goals and unexpected expenses that may crop up.

Let's take a look at some of the problems that affect retirement planning, and then we'll consider some possible solutions.

1. Many companies no longer offer pensions.
2. The social security fund is rapidly diminishing.
3. When you choose to start receiving your social security payments makes a difference.
4. Health issues are causing people to retire earlier than they had planned.
5. Banks are paying very low interest rates on savings accounts.
6. Many people have lost money on bad investments in the stock market.
7. People have lost their 401(k) plans due to bad management on the part of their employer.
8. People are unemployed and are therefore using all their savings to live on.

Here are some possible solutions to these problems:

Problem #1
Many companies no longer offer pensions.

Solution
You can set up your own pension in the form of an annuity. Later in the chapter we will discuss annuities in more detail.

Problem #2
The social security fund is rapidly diminishing.

Solution
Consider that social security benefits will only be one part of your retirement package. You can augment social security benefits with annuities, CDs, IRAs, 401(k) plans, stocks, bonds, mutual funds, a home-based business, or a reverse mortgage on your home. An explanation of these terms is listed on page 80.

Problem #3
When you choose to start receiving your social security payments makes a difference.

Solution
Let's say, for example, that if you take full retirement at age 66½, you will earn $1145.00.

If you take early retirement at age 62, you will only earn 73% of that social security income: $835.00.

But, if you can wait to age 70, you will earn an additional $320.00, for a total of $1465.00. So, if you are healthy, and can continue working until you are 70, it behooves you to do so!

Problem #4
Health issues are causing people to retire earlier than they had planned.

Solution
Adopt a vigorous lifestyle of healthy eating, proper water intake, moderate exercise, and reduced mental stress in order to remain healthy enough to continue working well into your 70s.

Problem #5
Banks are paying very low interest rates on savings accounts.

Solution
Consider investing in accounts paying a higher interest rate, like ones found at a credit union, investing in annuities, or investing in your life insurance policies, which all pay better interest rates than banks can offer.

Problem #6
Many people have lost money on bad investments in the stock market.

Solution
In a poor economy, investing in the stock market is not the best option, unless you have an investment counselor you know you can trust, and who has a proven track record of success.

Problem #7
People have lost their 401(k) plans (retirement savings plans) due to bad management on the part of their employer.

Solution #1
Consider using an IRA in place of the 401(k) plan.

Solution #2
If you are in your mid-50s and have an annual combined income of at least $80,000.00, you should be contributing at least 37% of your annual income to a retirement savings plan of some type in order to retire comfortably by age 65.

Problem #8
People are unemployed and are therefore using all their savings to live on.

Solution
If you own your own home, you have the option to get a reverse mortgage on your home.

Explanation of Terms Used in This Section

ANNUITY

According to the Merriam-Webster dictionary, an annuity is (1) a fixed sum of money paid to someone each year, typically for the rest of their life, (2) a form of insurance or investment entitling the investor to a series of annual sums.

An annuity is an insurance product that pays out income and can be used as part of a retirement strategy. There are different types of annuities, and a prudent investor must look at all the benefits offered by the annuity, and ask a lot of questions.

For example, before buying into an annuity you should ask these questions:

- Is the annuity backed by a large, secure insurance company?
- Does the annuity offer tax-deferred growth?
- Does the annuity offer a lifetime option? Does it offer you income you can't outlive?
- Does the annuity offer a high yield? The interest earning rate should offer a better interest rate than CDs.
- Does the annuity have flexible, penalty-free withdrawals?

How long must you wait to withdraw funds and what interest is charged for early withdrawal of funds?

- Does the annuity offer unlimited contributions, unlike a 401(K) fund?

- Can you pass the money on to a beneficiary if you pass away before you withdraw all the funds, helping your heirs to avoid probate?

These are some of the questions your insurance advisor should be able to answer to your satisfaction.

CD (CERTIFICATE OF DEPOSIT)

A CD is an interest-earning savings certificate that is federally insured by the FDIC. You can buy CDs worth different amounts. You promise to leave your CD in the bank or credit union for a specific period of time. This will earn you a guaranteed rate of interest on your money, in exchange for allowing the bank or credit union to "use" your money as an asset in order to earn interest for their institution. A CD pays a fixed rate for the fixed term and penalties are charged if you withdraw the funds before the term ends.

IRA

An IRA is a retirement savings account that is funded with your own money and earns interest. Generally speaking, you can begin to take your money out of your IRA without early-withdrawal penalties at age 59½.

401(K)

A 401(k) is a retirement savings plan offered through your

employer. The 401(k) offers you an opportunity to save money, and that money is usually matched in some part by your employer. You must invest for a certain amount of time before your employer contributes to the plan. This is known as "being vested" in the 401(k). Being "fully vested" means you have reached the time period (in years) in which your contributions are matched 100% by your employer. There have been a lot of horror stories about companies mismanaging these plans, so make sure your employer is reliable before you decide to invest your money in a 401(k).

Benefits of a 401(k): You get a tax break, since your contributions are withdrawn from your paycheck before taxes are withheld; the contributions from your employer are basically "free" money; and the dividends you earn are also tax deductible. Generally speaking, you can begin to take your money out of your 401(k) without early-withdrawal penalties at age 59½. After age 70½ you must start making minimum withdrawals or face heavy tax penalties.

STOCKS AND BONDS

The difference between stocks and bonds is that when you invest in stocks you are buying an interest in the profits of one particular company; stocks have no expiration date. A bond is issued for a specific period of time; bonds are basically a loan you are making to a company, government organization or other group in exchange for interest payments which will be paid out when the bond matures. When interest rates increase, bond prices usually fall.

MUTUAL FUND

A mutual fund is a pool of assets owned by many investors and operated by a management company. Mutual bonds may pay out a little less than stocks, but they are a bit safer because they don't depend on one individual company's assets, as stocks do.

A HOME-BASED BUSINESS

You may have a hobby or a skill you can turn into a home-based business. If you have the energy and drive to give it a try, start at your local city office to get your residential business license, set up your accounting system with easy-to-use software like QuickBooks, and start producing your product or offering your service. If you designate one room just for your business, you can deduct a portion of your rent/mortgage and utilities on your income taxes. You can deduct other business-related expenses, like phone calls, office supplies, supplies purchased to produce your product, and advertising.

REVERSE MORTGAGE ON YOUR HOME

If you own your own home and are at least 62 years old, the bank will loan you money on the equity of your home. It must be repaid when you sell the house, move out or pass away.

The negative impact of having a reverse mortgage occurs when your home's value becomes less than what you owe the bank (also known as your home being "under water"). Then, if you do need to move for any reason (unexpected divorce, or being unable to live in your own home due to illness or disability) and need to sell your home, you will not be able to sell it for enough money to pay off the loan from the bank. You could end up losing your home and still be in debt.

CREDIT UNION

"A credit union is a member-owned financial cooperative, democratically controlled by its members and operated for the purpose of promoting thrift, providing credit at competitive rates, and providing other financial services to its members."[9]

LIFE INSURANCE POLICY

A life insurance policy protects your loved ones from having to pay for your funeral expenses out of pocket, and it passes on some sort of financial security to your spouse or children after you pass away.

But insurance policies can also be an investment in your financial future, as they accrue earnings and pay dividends to your account that you can use when you need emergency funds.

There are different types of life insurance; some are designed to provide a benefit in the case of a specified event, typically a lump-sum payment. A common form of this design is term insurance.

Some are investment policies—where the main objective is to facilitate the growth of capital by regular or single premiums. The most common forms are whole life, universal life and variable life policies.

Finding a reputable life insurance specialist is crucial to providing yourself and your family financial security in the event of your death, or if you become disabled, become seriously ill, or simply want to securely invest in your retirement.

Sweet Senior Moments

There are a few perks to becoming a senior citizen; one of them is joining AARP, an advocacy group for senior citizens. AARP has information on aging, senior benefits, and programs offering reductions on insurance, to name a few. You can find AARP online at http://www.aarp.org.

When you go out to eat, ask the manager or your food server if there are reduced prices for seniors, and what hours and days they apply.

Another advocacy group, the National Council on Aging (NCOA), claims that over 20 billion dollars of benefits for older Americans with limited income is overlooked because people don't know where to find the benefits. Two more online resources to try are these:

1. BenefitsCheckUp at benefitscheckup.org.

2. Eldercare Locator at www.eldercare.gov, or call them toll-free at 800-677-1116 to find agencies and organizations that support senior citizens.

Glossary

BRAINSTORMING

Brainstorming can be done with a group of people, in which case it is a conference technique for solving specific problems, amassing information, stimulating creative thinking, and developing new ideas by unrestrained and spontaneous participation in discussion.

If you are brainstorming alone, take the time to set aside a place where you can relax and think freely, then let the ideas flow unimpeded, without trying to organize or prioritize them. *(See also the "Brainstorming Problems" section of this book.)*

INVESTMENTS VS. DISPOSABLE ASSETS

An investment is an item you buy that will become more valuable with time. Most of what we consider investments are actually disposable assets. For example, most people think jewelry is an investment, but it generally doesn't gain value as it gets older. Instead, its value is reduced, depending on the economy and the current value of the gold, diamonds or other precious stones in it.

However, if an asset still retains its value over time, it can be considered an investment. For example, cars are an investment, because if you maintain a car, you can still sell it after 10 years without total loss of value. According to Consumer Reports "your new vehicle depreciates at least 45% within the first three years," but after that time you can still get some value for it.

To see how much your used car is worth, check on the Kelley Blue Book website at http://www.kbb.com to see the value you could get from a dealer or from a private party. (A private party will pay you more than the dealer will.)

Make sure you have the car's make, model, year, and working condition, as well as engine size, how many cylinders the car has, and any improvements you've made to the car that may add value (such as installing a stereo, getting a custom paint job, and other amenities) in order to get an estimate for the car's worth. It's a real eye-opener!

About the Author

DIANE TEGARDEN is a self-made entrepreneur; her first company was a collection service for doctors which she called Save Em and Smile Collections Service. She operated the business from 1983–1984. Then Diane ran the finances for the security alarm company Digital Alarm Systems, which she co-owned with her husband Wade Webb from 1985–1995.

In 1995 she sold Digital Alarm Systems for a profit and with the money from the sale, she and her husband created a solar energy company, Solar Webb, Inc., which they started without borrowing a penny from the banks.

She was the CFO for Solar Webb, Inc. from 1995–2004, when she had to quit working due to a serious illness. After selling the business in 2004, Diane and Wade's finances experienced a severe drop in income—a 30% cut. They survived financially due to her experience with budgeting the expenses.

Once she regained her health in 2004, Diane formed her own small publishing company, FireWalker Publications, and has written and published three very different books:

How to Escape a Bad Marriage: A Self-Help Divorce Book for Women

Light Through Shuttered Window: A Compendium of My Poetry

Anti-Vigilante and the Rips in Time (a breakout sci-fi novel)

Budgeting on a Dime: 10 Steps to Financial Independence is her fourth book, to be followed by another poetry collection "Italian Bees Make Honey Pizza" (publication set for 2013).

Notes

[1] The Department of Energy | Energy Efficiency & Renewable Energy, pages cited were last modified August 10, 2012, http://www.fueleconomy.gov/feg/driveHabits.shtml/.

[2] The Department of Energy | Energy Efficiency & Renewable Energy, pages cited were last modified August 10, 2012, http://www.fueleconomy.gov/feg/maintain.shtml.

[3] The Department of Energy | Energy Efficiency & Renewable Energy, pages cited were last modified August 10, 2012, http://www.fueleconomy.gov/feg/driveHabits.shtml/.

[4] The Department of Energy | Energy Efficiency & Renewable Energy, pages cited were last modified August 10, 2012, http://www.fueleconomy.gov/feg/driveHabits.shtml/.

[5] The Department of Energy | Energy Efficiency & Renewable Energy, pages cited were last modified August 10, 2012, http://www.fueleconomy.gov/feg/driveHabits.shtml/.

[6] The Department of Energy | Energy Efficiency & Renewable Energy, pages cited were last modified August 10, 2012, http://www.fueleconomy.gov/feg/maintain.shtml.

[7] The Department of Energy | Energy Efficiency & Renewable Energy, pages cited were last modified August 10, 2012, http://www.fueleconomy.gov/feg/maintain.shtml.

[8] The Department of Energy | Energy Efficiency & Renewable Energy, pages cited were last modified August 10, 2012, http://www.fueleconomy.gov/feg/maintain.shtml.

[9] "Credit union." Wikipedia, The Free Encyclopedia, from the page last modified 17 July 2012 at 03:43, http://en.wikipedia.org/wiki/Credit_union. *See "View History" tab for list of authors.*

CPSIA information can be obtained
at www.ICGtesting.com
Printed in the USA
FSOW04n0450260615
8271FS